A PAT.

MW01599127

It was <u>awesome and so inspirational!</u>

Sandy T.

Thank you for *A Path of Peace with God.* You are on the path of healing and doing such wonderful work in the world.

Nelly B., Personal Assistant

I find your book of affirmations a remarkable effort. I have found these affirmations very helpful in guiding individuals and families through the throes of crises. Positive affirmations carefully selected from this fine book have helped those with whom I have worked bring into focus and manage their lives more effectively.

Bob H., retired college professor, consultant

Your book really brought it home to me. It is not just intellectual it is experiential. Sometimes reading just one sentence can turn your whole mood around. I would like to thank you for writing this book.

Lynn S., store owner

A friend told me about your book. I've read a lot of affirmation books. Yours is the best!

Nina C., artist

Your book really moved me! It has made a big impact in my life.

Phillip A.

Thank you for your exceptional book. It is life changing. It helped me to get back in touch with my soul and have a friendship with God.

Mona G., designer

About the Author

Drew Phillip Simmons, D.C. is a writer, doctor and spiritual seeker. He is dedicated to finding practical solutions to the obstacles keeping mankind from true spiritual abundance and physical health. As one member of our human family he feels a responsibility to contribute to the effort made by so many others working diligently to elevate our understanding of the planet and ourselves.

As a teenager in Los Angeles Dr. Simmons was deeply moved by the strong spirit of brotherhood and cooperation shared between people. He was a witness also to a great deal of physical and mental suffering and this impacted him tremendously. At the end of the school day he would frequently hike along the mountain trails behind his home searching his soul for answers. Atop mountain peaks often overlooking beautiful sunsets he thought long and hard. He wanted answers to the spiritual dilemmas posed by the great suffering around him but he also wanted to understand the cause of so many of the physical ailments in abundance. There was too much love and commitment for fear and ill health to have such an advantage and there were too many practical solutions available. He felt a duty and a responsibility to seek out effective solutions.

While attending college Dr. Simmons worked extensively with children. Over a period of six years he was both a teacher and a friend to hundreds of little ones. He taught them many lessons but they taught him many lessons as well. From them he learned about unconditional love and trust, playfulness, joyous curiosity and vulnerability. After many years of study, first in Los Angeles and later in northern California, he received his Bachelor of Arts degree in Psychology from Sonoma State University in 1993. It was time for him to take a new direction and he had to say good-bye to his friends and the beautiful place he called home.

After completion of physics and chemistry courses in San Francisco he began his chiropractic education across the bay in San Lorenzo. A passionate and serious student, he and a friend often visited a gigantic used bookstore in town buying up many of the books on health and healing. Evenings were frequently spent in Berkeley coffee shops studying alongside the local university students.

When it was possible, weekends were an opportunity to attend seminars taught by preeminent leaders in the fields of bodywork, nutrition and clinical practice. He was known for taking detailed notes in class and afterwards rewriting these notes into legible and easily understandable booklets that he and other classmates could then study from. Upon completion of his coursework and clinic hours in 1997 he was granted the Doctor of Chiropractic degree, Cum Laude, from Life Chiropractic College West.

Dr. Simmons lives and maintains a private practice in Los Angeles, California. He is well known for his successful approach to healing difficult and chronic cases including such disorders as migraine headaches, sciatica, bowel disease, spinal trauma and pain, sports injuries and immune dysfunction.

In addition to his extensive knowledge of the nervous system and musculoskeletal systems he also has a special interest in nutrition pathology and craniosacral dysfunction. He is widely sought out for his knowledge of nutrition and ability to diagnose nutrition-related disorders. Dr. Simmons welcomes feedback from readers on his book *A Path of Peace with God* and also on their experiences with health and healing.

How to Contact the Author

Please share your thoughts and feelings about *A Path* of *Peace with God*. Address your letter to the author in care of Fire of Faith Publications. We will make sure the author receives your correspondence. It cannot be guaranteed that the author will be able to respond to every letter received. Address your letter as follows:

> Drew Simmons, D.C.
> c/o Fire of Faith Publications
> 1204 Abbot Kinney Blvd.
> Venice, CA 90291

For a reply please include a self-addressed stamped envelope or provide us with your e-mail address. Thank you.

A
PATH OF PEACE
WITH GOD

A
PATH OF PEACE
WITH GOD

A Journey of Affirmations

Drew P. Simmons, D.C.

Fire of Faith Publications

Venice, California

Fire of Faith Publications
1204 Abbot Kinney Blvd.
Venice, CA 90291

Copyright © 1999 by Drew Phillip Simmons

All rights reserved. This book may not be reproduced in whole or in part, in any
form, without written permission from Fire of Faith Publications, except by a
reviewer, who may quote brief passages in a review.

 is a trademark of Fire of Faith Publications.

First Edition
First Printing, 2003

Cover design and interior layout by
Monica Leon Garrido

Simmons, Drew Phillip
A Path of Peace with God : A Journey of Affirmations / Drew Phillip Simmons

Library of Congress Control Number: 2002092860
ISBN 0-9722469-9-1

Printed in the United States of America

Note to Readers

Few things are more valuable than a committed relationship with a wise and trusted doctor. Without the benefit of such collaboration the state of the health can be left in jeopardy. Relying on symptoms such as pain as the main motivator to seek treatment is a poor policy. A large number of disorders can become very serious before any signs or symptoms are apparent. If detected early, many of these conditions are easily treatable. Do not wait for signs and symptoms to arise. Seeing a doctor, preferably holistic, periodically when you are healthy can improve the chances of staying healthy.

The information given in the following pages is profound and transformational but it is no substitute for personalized attention. It may seem noble to try and treat a problem without guidance but frequently it is quite foolish. The body and mind are complex and can require a great deal of detective work. This book has much wisdom but it is not a seasoned professional! Please be responsible and get the appropriate treatment for yourself when necessary.

Acknowledgments

It is by the grace of God that this book was made possible. To him I offer sincere thanks. My mother Audrey and my father Robert have been unwavering in their support of this undertaking. I truly appreciate and give thanks to both of you. The host of individuals who have offered their encouragement and excitement has been enormous. This has sustained me and brought me great joy. Thank you.

To my family, friends and patients, I would like to thank you for your continued enthusiasm and patience. I know that this project has taken a long time to complete and I am very grateful for your steadfast endurance.

There are two people who deserve special mention. The advice and wisdom of Louis Hay is life-changing. Without it I do not know where I would be. You have changed me like no other. It is through the persistent efforts of another very special person, Monica Leon Garrido, that the material presented in this book is made available to all. Thank you for your love and also your creative contribution by designing my book. We did it!

Author's Preface

Something very powerful and miraculous happened during the summer of 1997. It began one month after I had graduated from chiropractic college during a period of recuperation. The education was enlightening and rewarding but also very demanding. Years spent in class, endless nights studying for examinations with little sleep and long hours treating very sick patients were just some of the many challenges. The experience left me thoroughly exhausted, frustrated and angry with God and the world. In the flash of an instant all this negativity and frustration would disappear.

It began the night of July 14. The internal tension had been building to a climax. Even after graduation the anxiety and desperation of all the endless hurdles to jump remained with me. I yearned to free myself from the lingering negative emotions and thoughts. It was then that I picked up a very special book. For a long time it had been lying around but never had I taken the time to read it. The time was ripe for the messages contained within it to penetrate and transform me.

I read several pages into the first chapter and have never been the same since. The book *You Can Heal Your Life* by Louise Hay was the catalyst I did not know I was looking for. Just a short way into the first chapter I came face to face with a choice: continue the mental and emotional self-destruction and anguish or turn to a new way? I saw my opportunity and I took it.

No longer could I continue the stubborn cycle of frustration that had become such a usual part of my inner world. I resolved never to go back. There was some fear and uneasiness knowing that I was abandoning so many of my thoughts. I felt a new and unfamiliar joy, and also a deep sense of relief, at leaving behind a painful path and starting on a better yet still uncharted direction.

There was only one way I would be able to systematically halt the barrage of negative thoughts and feelings. Continuous repetition of affirmations was my only escape route. I would have to mentally repeat affirmations during the entire time that I was awake. It was daunting to realize that I would have to force myself to do this the entire summer and possibly longer if I was to extinguish my negative thoughts. This is what it was going to take to dramatically repattern my thinking. Halting the flow of affirmations would have been like pouring water over a campfire on a chilly night. Very quickly they became a constant compulsion of mine.

There was little choice but to endure my own self-imposed mental marathon. I could no longer tolerate the internal pain generated by negative thinking. Never would I allow more than several seconds of uncontrolled, habitual thinking to occur. The fear of slipping back to the old way would always immediately compel me to again repeat an affirmation. Any slight negative thought would immediately trigger repetition. Whether I was waking up in the morning, falling asleep, conversing with others, eating or doing any other activity I forced myself to inwardly repeat my own constructed phrases.

At times I would repeat a single affirmation for days on end. The procedure I developed for creating and repeating the affirmations, called "The Method", is described in the introduction. With the newfound book, my decision to change, and the tool of affirmation I began a new life.

That first evening I made the hardest decision of my life: to stay at peace with God. It was time to let go of all of the perpetual inner argument, valid or not, that was keeping me from this commitment. With a little embarrassment I gave thanks to God and turned over to sleep, hoping my resolve would be as strong next morning.

Upon waking the next day I immediately reconfirmed my new commitment. Quickly I rushed to a lush and secret spot alongside a stream in the Pacific Palisades Highlands. There I sat on a rock next to a series of beautiful little waterfalls. Steadily and end-lessly I repeated affirmations both out loud and in my head. I was afraid that if I stopped, the negative thoughts might once again consume me. There was a newness and a freshness within me and around me as I discovered how powerful repeating positive affir-mations could be. I was finding a new direction with God and leaving old negativity behind.

To maintain this place of joy with God I realized that I would have to examine all of my behaviors under a magnifying glass. Any behavior toward others that could potentially increase their anxiety or negativity would have to be omitted. This meant avoiding all arguments, not being critical, not making disapproving gestures or comments and not talking negatively about anyone. It meant showing understanding or approval to others for their ideas and also giving out many compliments. I would have to exclude all of my actions that had a potential for bringing up divisiveness. To upset others would have dramatically interfered with my own effort to keep spirited.

It was on this first day, when I ventured out of the hidden sanctuary for a lunch break at the nearby village, that I felt the strong presence of God. This was thoroughly new and unfamiliar to me. It did not feel as though he was visiting me personally. The presence felt similar to seeing a robust grandfather who was somewhat busy and on his way toward a destination. The feeling was strong but fleeting. I determined that I should never lose sight of this perception so I began to make a habit of sensing this grandfatherly presence around me.

Also this first day in the hills I began to feel powerful energy surging within me and around me. I knew that this was a pivotal time in my life. There was fear and trepidation that I might fall back into old ways but there was also excitement and exuber-ance. Like walking along the edge of a steep precipice – as long as you keep on the path you will be O.K. No longer could I afford to waste precious energy courting negative thoughts and feelings.

Today was the day to start learning how to better conserve and control my energy.

I wrote my affirmations down and soon began to suspect that a book was developing. A pen and a little notebook never left my side and many a new affirmation came up even before I opened my eyes in the morning. I dutifully recorded these cherished affirmations one after the other and they appear here in this book in the same order that they arose.

One day in November, as I was repeating an affirmation on the rock, a mountain lion came to visit me. The lion was travelling up the stream when she came around a bend and practically ran into me. Many minutes passed with each of us in mortal fear of the other. Our eyes stayed locked for what seemed like an eternity. We were in very close quarters. There was a steep mountain wall on one side of the stream and dense foliage on the other. She would either have to turn around and go back down stream the way she came or come directly at me. I glanced away briefly and, after wondering if this would be my last move, I looked back to see that she had disappeared. I did not spend a lot of time at the rock after that.

For another year I continued to dwell constantly on affirmations. Slowly over time I felt less of a need to rely on them. My near certainty that they would eliminate my negative thought patterns was correct. Many of the affirmations became etched indelibly into my mind.

Read this chronicle of affirmations, as a novel is read, starting at page one. To jump to different sections out of context would be like reading a book or watching a movie by starting in the middle first. Similarly, to have reorganized these affirmations into chapters based on their subject would be like forcing people to live together just because they look alike. If you would like to find an affirmation on a particular subject please refer to the extensive index.

Never was there an effort to deliberately produce material for a book. Each affirmation came up as part of a naturally unfolding process and was developed spontaneously. This is the record of my personal transformation and the affirmations I created to chart a new course of thought for myself.

Drew Simmons
Los Angeles, California
July, 2002

Introduction

One day while sitting on a rock in a lush little paradise I devised a powerful method of mind control. It happened on July 15, 1997 the day after I resolved to give up my negative outlook. Far from being a method to deceive others, the goal of this procedure is to control the mind of oneself!

When the mind is restless and chaotic it is not healthy. Whether it has gotten to this place from trauma, abuse, toxins, negative or confused thinking or just plain bad luck it needs to be tamed. We can let our thoughts take control of us or we can take control of our thoughts if we know how. The procedure presented here, called "The Method", offers the option of choosing our thoughts. Those people whose minds are not chaotic and restless should still concern themselves with learning the supreme skill – mastering the thoughts.

How can there be free will if there is no knowledge of how to direct the thoughts? How can there be true freedom and free will if one cannot even reroute their own thought processes away from harmful and unhealthy thoughts? Piloting the mind away from injurious thinking should be considered a basic necessity and a prerequisite to lasting freedom and free will.

Without food the body cannot live and without the knowledge of how to keep the thoughts composed, mental and emotional happiness cannot be sustained. The procedure supplied here, or one similar, is no less than a necessity since it gives the strength to either withstand or steer clear of inner harm and hold fast instead to inner health.

To do the technique you will need to purchase only one item. That item is the tool of affirmation and the cost is in time and dedication to mental exercise. This procedure builds the mind up as exercise builds the body up. By directing our thoughts we also gain influence over our emotions. In this way we can direct our emotions instead of allowing our emotions to direct us.

For some just reading or periodically reviewing affirmations is enough, but for others a more intense and involved procedure to thoroughly transform the thinking habits is needed. The affirmations in this book are for everybody. The procedure presented in this introduction may be needed only by certain people or at certain times.

First, be aware of which thoughts are constructive and which are destructive. Examples of injurious thinking include blame, criticism, judgement, hostility, aggression and cynicism to name just a few. Some examples of constructive thinking are co-operation, appreciation, patience, forgiveness, respect and optimism. Know which of your thoughts are working against you and which are working for you.

Determine whether the destructive thoughts are about oneself or others. Some people direct most of their negative thoughts and feelings toward themselves. They are filled with self-blame and self-criticism. Other people feel it is everybody but themselves that is the problem. Most people are probably somewhere in between. Know when you are the brunt of your own negativity and know when you have reserved it for others. The situations are different and often need to be addressed differently.

All negative thoughts and feelings are branches of one master negative emotion: fear. Whether certain negative thoughts or emotions are justified or not they are fear. Fear carries with it negativity and often these two terms can be used interchangeably. The master positive emotion is love. We hold onto our fears but they keep us from our love and the strength it offers. For every fear within us love has a counterpart that is also contained within us. Our inner fear is of our own inner loving strength.

Fear can come up either slowly, quickly or it may be there all of the time. For example, you may be feeling quite fine and then thoughts of your overdue taxes arise, causing you immediate grief and guilt. It is quite clear in this instance when a state of fear has been entered. In another case you may feel quite fine at the start of a debate with a friend over politics but afterwards you notice you have become depressed. It was less clear when the fear began during this case but still it is there. Perhaps the thoughts and feelings are painful or uncomfortable almost all of the time. This is a situation where fear is easier to identify because it is there constantly. At those times when you are not mentally or emotionally comfortable consider it possible that fear is present.

The body can help tell you when the state of fear has been entered. If you notice such reactions as your jaw clenching, your hands clenching, your smile turning to a frown or muscles tightening, the body is possibly responding to fear. A clenching of one's jaw or hands can be an immediate and accurate indicator of the presence of fear in the body. Each person is unique in the way her or his body will respond to fear. Monitor how your body responds to fear when it comes up. Learning its responses will help signal to you when the state of fear has been entered.

To stop the cycle of fear in the mind you must stop the cycle of fear in the body. Do not allow the body to maintain its fearful postures especially while repeating affirmations. I never permit myself to keep my jaw or hands clenched. Keeping the jaw and hands open and relaxed helps keep fear out of the body and greatly assists the mind in keeping fear away.

Spot fear immediately so it can be quickly discarded or eradicated. If it is not spotted and managed quickly it can spread like a wildfire. A larger fire does more damage and is harder to put out. A little bit of fear unchecked can swamp the mind just as sure as a drip from a leaky roof can soak a house. As an airplane pilot routinely monitors the gauges to make sure the plane is flying properly and on the right course, monitor the mind and the body frequently and keep it on course. With practice checking gauges becomes instinctive for the pilot and with practice sensing fear and negativity becomes instinct for the mind. The cost of living in fear is too steep to not do it.

Once the fearful thought or emotion is noticed, identify the specific brand. Just as light can be divided into colors, and darkness can be divided into shades of gray, fear has its many expressions. First, is it negativity directed toward oneself or another? Second, name it for what it is: blame, anger, a grudge, addiction, attachment to the past, betrayal, criticism, cynicism, etc. Each of these is just one type, one expression, of fear.

Construct an affirmation that gives you power and confidence over the fear. Choose whether you want to include the particular type of fear you have identified or avoid it. Many people suggest avoiding the mention of anything negative in affirmations. I, on the other hand, have frequently included the type of fear identified within the affirmation.

When fear is exposed it loses its power. It is calling a spade a spade. Like a criminal that has been caught in the act, naming one's fear is the first step to overcoming it. In another example, when a doctor correctly identifies a disorder the power of the corruption is reduced. Being able to find and identify the problem is an important step in solving the problem. Some examples of completed affirmations that recognize and own up to one's fear are, "I choose to let go of all grudges right now," or, "Now is not a time to start blaming myself."

Make the affirmation refer to the present. The first affirmation above illustrates this by ending with the word "now" and the second example also shows this by beginning with, "Now is not a time to." There is no time like the present to start getting rid of fear and including a word such as "now" helps assure an immediate reaction by the mind.

Use the general word "fear" or name the type of fear specifically. For example, imagine that you are both resentful and angry with a boss for requiring that you complete a very difficult project in a short period of time. A good affirmation might be, "I hereby let go of all fear toward others that is keeping me from total success." In this example the all-encompassing word "fear" is used instead of the specific feelings of resentment and anger. It is a choice whether to include the specific fear identified or use a general word such as "fear" or "negativity."

At certain times it may feel best to avoid altogether any reference to negative concepts within the affirmation. For example, someone has just upset you. One affirmation might be, "I am at peace with all others on this day." Another one might be, "Now is not a time to bring myself down because of how others are." In neither of these affirmations is fear, negativity or any of their variations mentioned. The goal is a feeling of power over, and release of inner fear. It is the shift away from the unpleasant feeling to a better feeling that tells you the affirmation is effective. If an affirmation does not grab you find another one that does.

Feelings of embarrassment and shame for saying positive affirmations are pure fear and self-defeat. Ignore all such blocks to advancement or say an affirmation to cast them out. Example, "I immediately cast out all negative feelings that do not deserve to be a part of me."

Repetition of the affirmations is the key. Dwell on the same affirmations over time. Thinking the same old negative thought over and over again is a negative thought pattern. Plant new thoughts by dwelling on positive thoughts over and over. Do it at necessary moments and do it over time as well. Temporary use will bring short-term good feeling while long-term use will bring long-term gain.

Even if you forget positive thoughts, condemn them or devalue them, eventually you will have to come back to them. There is no other alternative to fear. Do not rely on others to keep you happy and mentally strong. Producing strong and positive thoughts at will provides immunity from the emotional swings of others.

Keep training the mind to shun fear and it will lose its habit for it. Reprioritize so that ridding oneself of fear is paramount to all other petty concerns. The ability to shed fear quickly and remain positive is a good marker of mental strength and advancement.

Have a working set of affirmations that you can draw upon. Have multiple ones memorized for each fear that has taken you down in the past.

Know how to create new affirmations. Like disease in the body, fear has a near endless number of variations. Have numerous different ways of phrasing an affirmation. Just as fear can throw a variety of similar punches, have a variety of similar affirmations in response.

Do not hesitate to repeat two or more affirmations together. This complicates the mind and forces it to forget its fear faster. It is this type of mental will-power that will overpower fear's influence permanently.

The mind will not want to give up its fear unless there is good reason. Two affirmations means that there are twice as many reasons for the mind to give up its affair with fear. Example: Your lover has just broken up with you. Start focusing your abilities with alternating affirmations such as, "I let others move out of my life if need be." " I know I will be fine."

It is not all joy and happiness that affirmations are supposed to bring up. Sometimes the best affirmation is the one that brings up the fear. You may actually feel your fear exiting your body. Just keep repeating it. Light and dark cannot exist in the same space together.

Keep your affirmations to yourself. Do not keep the good news of affirmations to yourself but it may be best to be private in how you use them. It can look strange and turn people off if they see you talking to yourself. Unable to read your thoughts, they will be unable to detect your private mental activity. Affirmations give you the hidden advantage.

Use the power and energy of sound to stamp in the affirmation. This means sometimes stating the affirmations out loud so that every cell of your body knows your intention to expunge the negativity within. We express our fear verbally so express the controlled force of affirmation verbally. We aim to reprogram all habits and that means speech too. Do not just keep affirmation bottled within. A little bit of private time devoted to out-loud repetition will go a long way.

Negativity can come up at any time... so too should affirmation. Do not relegate affirmations to only one particular time during the day. Make sure they are on hand at all times. Affirmations, as they are presented here, are really planned positive thoughts designed to overwhelm and replace negative thoughts and fear. Repeat them whenever and wherever negativity arises including while bathing, eating, studying, driving, walking, conversing, waking up, going to sleep and all other activities. Stick with a single affirmation for minutes, hours or even days but eventually try other ones too. Don't forget your good ones.

In some rare cases full immersion in affirmations may be called for. From the instant you awaken to the instant you fall asleep you will repeat affirmations – no exceptions! Even while you sleep you will find yourself in repetition. This book is the product of such a situation. Ideally, for this level of devotion, you will have plenty of time to yourself and also a sanctuary somewhere in nature where you can slip away often.

Undermining fear requires precise timing. Each time it appears it should be met head on. Fear is persistent so we will have to be even more persistent. Remember, immediately identify any negative thoughts and feelings that intrude upon your positive state and classify them as fear. It makes no difference whether your fear or negativity about the matter is well-founded. Priority one is to re-establish a happy and content state. Fear will do its best to cloud your judgement and make you think it is bigger than it is. It has only as much power as you give it.

Gauge the level of threat the fear presents. If it is a low level of fear presenting no threat you may be able to safely forget it. If you have little tolerance for any fear, or if it is a medium or high level of fear, rely on support measures such as affirmation and do not succumb to the fear. One way to gauge the level of fear is by recognizing the amount of anxiety the negative thought or feeling causes you. A medium or high level of fear should always be actively neutralized and a low level of fear often needs management also.

Fear is not a big problem... *it is the biggest problem!* It will take far more than affirmation and "The Method" to short-circuit it. Throw too much at it, not too little. Affirmations are the foundation, but it will take more, much more.

Fear is very efficient at creating great division within a person, between people and between races. It is difficult to see, especially in oneself, and it is even more difficult to get rid of. Affirmation, as a tool to control thought and influence emotion, is a big missing part of the puzzle but it is not the only part. If this formidable opponent is to be overcome, affirmation must be coordinated with numerous other effective methods. The place to take fear on is within oneself. Teach others through example.

Coordinate the effort to overcome fear by taking a holistic approach. Know the three major components of the person: mental, chemical and structural. This holistic model has been termed the Triad of Health by Applied Kinesiologists.

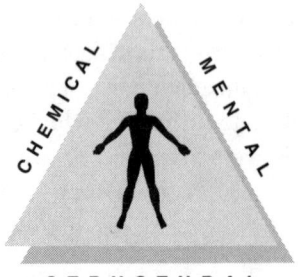 **Triad of Health**

"Mental" refers to the thoughts and emotions, "chemical" refers to the biochemical processes occurring in the body, and "structural" refers to the underlying skeleton, joints and soft tissues of the body. A weakness in any one of these three areas will create susceptibility to fear and illness. In chronic conditions all three components will have an imbalance. Many people have at least two of the components in need of attention. Know which of these three major categories require support.

Rely on a skilled holistic healer for guidance. Do not make the mistake of thinking you can do it all yourself. Be aware that most health-care providers are not holistic. Such practitioners prefer instead to address her or his area of specialization only.

For example, psychologists, counselors, ministers and psychics typically concern themselves only with the mental component. A nutritionist is working with the biochemistry as is the general practitioner prescribing pharmaceutical drugs. Most dentists, chiropractors, orthopedists and podiatrists are focused squarely on structure. If the healer is non-holistic it may be necessary to see additional practitioners skilled in other areas. The tool of affirmation supports the mental component of the Triad of Health and used alone is not holistic. Make sure your mind and body are getting the support they need.

There are many supportive measures that greatly compliment affirmations – use them. Do not wait for a problem to develop. Build and strengthen all three divisions of the Triad of Health even when they are healthy.

Flower essences are potent catalysts that work on the mental component. It is wise to use these concurrently with affirmations. Flower essences are not essential oils. They work at a deep level to bring out our strengths and limit our weaknesses and susceptibility to fear.

The chemical component of our body is greatly supported by a wholesome diet and properly prescribed nutritional supplements.

Effective bodywork is what it will take to restore and maintain a strong and stable structure. Chiropractic, with its emphasis on the nervous system, is a potent way of influencing all the structural elements of the body. If there is altered function within the soft tissues supporting and enveloping the brain and spinal cord it may be necessary to utilize craniosacral techniques. Each of the above procedures yields great rewards when diagnosed and administered correctly.

Make sure all sides of the Triad of Health are treated concurrently. It takes power to overcome fear and illness and using a strong holistic program gives that power. A healing protocol is stronger when it addresses the structure, the chemistry and the mind simultaneously. Any delay or lack of coordination gives the adversary an advantage. Do not give fear an advantage by letting illness sink its roots in.

If there has been long-term fear and negativity the brain chemistry and physiology may have actually changed to make easier the transmission of its negative messages. This is because our brain becomes more efficient at the activities we repeat over and over. For example, playing a musical instrument or typing at a keyboard becomes easy with practice. If we frequently think and feel negative then the brain will become efficient at transmitting these messages too. *The Method helps rewire the brain so that it is efficient at transmitting positive messages.*

Changing thought will be a momentous undertaking for some people. To train the mind to consistently return to a positive direction can be like taking down a house and building another one in its place. Initially, a great deal of work might be needed but once the new structure is in place less frequent "maintenance" work may be all that is required (i.e., shorter periods of affirmation repetition and other supportive procedures). The Method is a realistic way to truly produce lasting change in thought as well as in the brain itself. Here is a step by step breakdown of it:

1) Promptly identify when the thoughts and/or emotions have become fearful/negative.(The Method can be used at any time even when no fear is present.)

2) Make sure the hands and jaw are relaxed and open. The biting surfaces of the teeth should not be touching. The tip of the tongue can be kept between the upper and lower front teeth as a reminder to keep the teeth apart.

Relax all other areas of the body that have tightened due to fear and negativity.

3) Choose or create an affirmation that brings a feeling of relief from the discomfort of the inner negativity. Two affirmations repeated together may be better than one. Write your good ones down now so you do not forget them.

4) Repeat the affirmation(s) inwardly or out loud while at the same time periodically making sure that no part of the body is tightening up.

5) Consider taking some drops of flower essences immediately when the fear is recognized or when repetition is started. If you have other supportive measures consider incorporating them as well.

6) After several seconds or minutes evaluate whether the affirmation chosen is having the desired effect. If not try other ones.

7) Repeat the affirmation(s) as long as you need to. Do not feel embarrassed if repetition lasts a long time.

8) Periodically review whether the fear has subsided. Decide to (a) stop repetition and resume the normal thought process, (b) choose another affirmation, or (c) continue repeating the same affirmation. If some activity of daily living, or your own thoughts, temporarily interfere with repetition do not blame yourself or others. Continue repetition at the next available opportunity.

9) If the decision is to stop then congratulate yourself on a job well done. Resolve to stay committed to a positive way of being. Resolve to see the fear when it arises, to not give in to the fear, and to return to the tool of affirmation when necessary. Give thanks where it is due.

With dedication an entirely new thought pattern can result. If negative thought patterns are deeply ingrained it will not necessarily be easy. An immediate shift to a positive state can occur by repeating an affirmation, but changing the mind so that positive thoughts are the natural tendency is a different matter. Thinking itself is a habit. Trying to change poor thought is no less than trying to change a long-term bad habit. Making affirmations a habit will help end the cycle of negative thoughts and the painful feelings that accompany them.

Never leave the mind without guiding principles. Just as a scientist adheres to the scientific method, or a lawyer conforms to legal procedure, make sure the mind has a plan to stick to. Never stray far from a sound policy that assures the mind continued health and happiness. If the arrangement does not encourage mental strength and prudent conduct in times of adversity, find another one that does. Know what the underlying plan is and if there is none find or devise one.

This work is a personal constitution. The primary fundamental guideline has already been illustrated. This first indispensable guiding principle is: always have a procedure that brings order to the thoughts if they become chaotic. The technique detailed in this introduction, The Method, fulfills that basic need. There are many other guidelines and these are shown by the affirmations offered throughout the following pages.

You will notice repetition of some ideas. As previously explained, it is repetitiveness that really retrains the mind. Positive thinking is not just talked about, it is demonstrated first hand through example.

Here is a manual, a reference tool and a prayer book. Its many practical insights and ideas for healthy treatment of oneself and others make it a manual. The many thousands of positive affirmations covering hundreds of different subjects make it a valuable reference book. Its unbridled and unending devotion to God and Spirit makes it worthy of consideration as a book of prayer. I hope you will enjoy it.

I accept life's challenge and know that I am protected.

Yesterday my old self died!

I watch my footsteps carefully so I do not go into negative patterns.

I release any need to blame God or others.

I thank God and all others who have helped me to create a spectacularly wonderful life.

I freely express gratitude toward God and the world.

I accept that the incidents of my past have been a consequence of my own actions.

I thank God for my beautiful life, my family and the success I revel in now.

I am not betraying my old self by following a new path.

I accept responsibility for my past thoughts and actions and the effects these have had on my life.

Anger and frustration is a response pattern. I choose to transform these patterns through new thoughts and actions.

I do not blame myself for the choices I have made in the past.

I release any need to judge and criticize others.

I have been setting myself up for this transformation my whole life.

My new way of peace and transformation is through: acceptance, gratitude, release, understanding, new thoughts, new behaviors.

I have been supported and protected by God.

I praise God for the good that life has to offer. I praise myself for obtaining these good things and I do not blame God for what happens to me in the world.

I trust God and know that he helps protect me.

God's love and help continue even when man intervenes.

God actively assists me in my life.

I realize how perplexed I was and let this knowledge affirm the true correctness of the path I am now on.

It is a new time now.

I want others to read of this transformation I am creating for myself.

A Path of Peace with God

I cannot afford to blame others right now.

There is a huge amount of support lifting me.

This is the perfect time and place for me to do this.

I am not in a position to be casting any blame right now.

I thank others often since so much is done for me.

No cynicism,
No criticism,
No clenched jaw antagonism.

This is a time of tranquility, peace and abundance.

I avoid all inner and outer name-calling.

A look in the eye makes a "thanks" so much better.

A Path of Peace with God

Beauty perceived outside is love being felt on the inside.

It is joyous to share in this new embrace of love and acceptance.

I extend great thanks to the people and places around me.

I walk with a smile on my face and in my heart.

I breathe in a new understanding of old destructive ways.

I keep letting the God force back in.

I keep lifting up and staying up and giving the opportunity to do so to others.

I project good spirit to those around me.

I am creating an entirely new way of being for myself...
and a new way of communicating with others.

I shall keep discovering the things in life that strengthen my
new way of being.

I feel a deep common bond to everyone around me.

How close I might have come to missing this transformation!

I will never go back to the old way.

The freshness of my thoughts is mirrored in the freshness of the
world around me.

I share with others the happiness I am creating for myself.

I dispel old critical ways and bring in a new thoughtful way.

I let go of any impatience within myself.

Staying delicate.

I talk often of personal transformation with others.

Dragonflies, butterflies and birds stay close to me when I am in nature.

Right now I seek only to change myself.

It is great that I can share this moment with You.

God's brilliant radiance finally pushed its way into my awareness.

Every morning I acknowledge our partnership, my new awareness and the satisfaction I receive with You at my side.

It is a new day in this new awareness.

As I keep this up I am gaining greater and greater momentum.

I very openly thank people and give many compliments.

God forms a synchrony of movement before my eyes.

My life is a vigorous expression of love and gratitude.

I see God's joyful effort in the people and things around me.

I feel the depth and sincerity of others and this lifts me to higher and higher heights.

I cast no blame.

I am with others where they are.

I easily let go of the past.

I choose thoughts consciously and carefully.

I am at peace.
I am protected.
And I am safe.

I have no resistance to letting the past go.

I release any need to make more out of a situation than is necessary.

I easily resolve difficulties that arise.

I release any abrasiveness.

I am not drawn into arguments.

I see clearly if people feel wronged by me and I work quickly to bring resolve.

I resolve problems peacefully.

I do not react to hostility.

I see the validity of what people say.

I gather great momentum in this new endeavor.

I feel truly fulfilled by my knowledge of God.

Blaming others undermines the strength and the power I have to control my life.

I hereby illuminate the spark I have within me to connect, acknowledge, repair, rescind, relieve.

I feel the warmth of Spirit protection and assistance and see this in everything that I do.

I allow myself to receive fully the great joy and love in the world.

I move about the world totally free and unencumbered.

I release any fear that keeps me from fully exploring and expressing this great space with all others.

I go about the world completely confident and free to express this new way of being.

I maintain total freedom as I move through the world.

I thank God for my past and what it has allowed me to accomplish now.

I acknowledge and understand what others have to say.

A Path of Peace with God

I cherish this great place of inner joy, acceptance, power and laughter.

I breathe in only acceptance for a while.

I now give thanks where it is due.

I gather great momentum as I travel to places I never thought possible.

I made this transformation happen!

Repeating an affirmation is nothing short of pure mind control.

Small shift in awareness...
great leaps from old patterns.

A crow's call reminds the old self to stay with the way of the new.

I let go of all fear that I will lose this place of mental peace.

This is still so beautifully new.

I go around confidently in this new state of mind.

Responding negatively just isn't good enough anymore.

I delight in other people's delight.

I look up toward God and heaven often.

This sense makes sense later on too.

I let go of any need to interpret things negatively.

I do not lose this place of mental peace.

A Path of Peace with God

I give myself the greatest of all gifts.

I delight completely in happy experiences.

I get a knowing smile when I spot God in the world.

I am very happy giving many thanks and praising God.

There is a new level of personal responsibility for me.

I will not blame God. I will not blame myself. And I will not blame others.

I will be careful with the thoughts I obey or they might just take me the wrong way.

I discard whatever I must and see clearly how vulnerable I am.

I release any attachment to my past and begin this new day in total awareness of God.

I see the many ways that I am helped by others.

I keep praising myself for maintaining this spirited place.

As I read these affirmations they move throughout my entire being.

I get on a roll each morning thinking and saying these affirmations.

I am a spontaneous affirmation generator!

I follow others easily into their own brand of joy and happiness.

I see the love in our laws and how they help bring us together.

There is triumph and victory in our togetherness.

Music and laughter lift me to the happy place I am reaching for.

I am not afraid to go to the highest heights.

I hear birds chirping and singing with laughter and gaiety encouraging me along on this positive path.

I cast out any fear of negative thoughts.

These affirmations are answers to long-standing personal riddles.

Thank You for the many signs of Your love.

Total thanks.
Total acknowledgments.
Total acceptance.
No blame.

I feel a deeper tenderness than I have ever known.

I have to emphasize what I only mildly cherished before.

I cast out any need to respond aggressively.

I release any need to be reactive.

I seal in this new way.

I do not stay on what is negative for very long at all.

A Path of Peace with God

The little acts people do to come together are vast and many.

I observe and illuminate the care and concern to get a true picture.

Our concern for each other and yearning to be free is intense and all-pervasive.

I feel when energy rises within me and I let it lift me higher and higher.

I let go of all blame and give to others the benefit of the doubt.

I never leave the grace with You I know to be true.

God's support is continuously manifest for me.

I have everything I need right now.

I see God in the sky and feel him close to my side.

I feel a deep confidence within me knowing God's strength is behind me.

I let others be in the space they are in.

It is no use being angry with others.

I walk in gratitude for that which is around me.

I know of God's intelligence in the timing of all things and interactions.

I am focused on looking up and not down.

Everything around me reflects with great synchrony God's majestic kingdom.

I see through the veil of negative thought to the great underlying desires of bonding and community.

I feel the excitement of this new state of mind.

I accept God as an undeniable aspect of my life.

I interpret things in ways that increase my strength and power.

I step out of the madness and see great truth.

I will not blame.
I will not criticize.
And I will not be angry.

I am blessed this day and completely illuminated by God's light.

I do all actions thoughtfully and with love.

Throughout this day I feel fully the true sea of support and freedom surrounding me.

Today I am lifted to a place of even newer and brighter awareness.

I know that God's work and full understanding are behind what I see before me.

I give out many compliments and see when good things happen.

I do not feel resentment today.

I see clearly and acknowledge fully the frequent help that I am given.

I go forth with full faith, trust and knowledge in the world.

I walk with new knowledge when I sense an old doubt.

I continually breathe in God's great spirit today.

No blame.
No judgment.
No criticism.

I see the great assistance that we provide each other.

There is great joy, intensity and endless reciprocity between us.

God awareness moves me higher and higher.

I feel the breath that creates new life.

Today I receive total protection and total insight.

We are at peace together.

I am adventuring into brand new realms.

Speaking of the best in things only lifts me higher.

I am acutely aware of God's powerful energy in myself and others.

I keep the rhythm going at a high rate.

What happened in the past is done. No use dwelling on it now!

I find happiness from no blame, no criticism, many thanks and many blessings.

The majesty of nature instructs me on God's true peace.

I bless any old destructive thought and nod in new understanding.

I let others go the way that suits them.

I see clearly the good things I do for myself.

I enjoy others fully and without criticism.

I sit in acceptance of God and all people.

I never hesitate to change what I need to change to be fully happy.

I see God's beauty in everything around me.

I release any hostility and bring in new acceptance.

I let others just be instead of judging them.

I feel truly rewarded.

A Path of Peace with God

I release any feelings of being shortchanged by the world.

I give myself the gift of a lifetime.

I earned this.

This is my greatest accomplishment.

This is the greatest thing I could do for myself.

No blame. No shame.

I derive power from the world around me.

I understand people's troubles but do not feel the depths with them.

I move forward under great power.

A Path of Peace with God

I am happy where I am right now.

No shutting myself off inside.
No cutting myself off inside.

I release rigidity. I release all inner restrictions.

I announce my faith and devotion throughout all planes of exis-
tence!

There is great joy in acknowledging what I really know to be
true!

I feel intense pleasure and satisfaction today.

I am thinking often of this move into higher heights.

I do not at all engage in arguments or debates.

I have great strength to move freely past the fears of yesterday.

Today I know a joy I have never known before.

I see a true sensitivity in everyone around me.

I am totally happy and content in the space I have created.

I have wonderful insights and see the incredible things that happen to me today.

I am confident and at peace with myself.

I cherish the great gifts of joy I am given.

No blame. No judgment. No criticism.
These are my mantras of freedom.

I easily let negative thoughts go as I move into a free and clear place.

I see the many ways that God's love shines through to me.

I cast out all doubt keeping me from full acceptance of God.

I feel no trace of resentment or anger.

I have succeeded totally in establishing this new healthier way.

I did incredibly well under the circumstances.

Today I make it happen!

I do what it is I must do now.

I change even the deepest habits… my thoughts.

I know that I will not get what I want through anger and re-sentment.

Negative feelings I cast out completely.

I am happy that I have attained this joyous knowledgeable state.

I am growing younger and healthier with these new ideas.

I continually re-affirm the global all-pervasive good.

I do not let thoughts of a world in conflict generate negativity within myself.

I continually refine my ways of seeing God in the world.

I know God is the backdrop to all situations.

I access resolution and mutual understanding anywhere at any-time.

I do not give power away by dwelling on old events.

Seeing anger in others reminds me to keep a place of concern and cooperation.

Today I remain in a place of understanding.

What does not work for me: blame, criticism, self-hate, God-rejection.

I keep powerful now.

I attract great love and beauty to myself.

Things are completely perfect for me right now.

I brush off the negative and stay with what is positive.

I consciously choose this path of freedom.

I see the care that people express for each other.

I stand tall in no judgement and no blame.

There is no other way for me now.

I am not drawn in by the seductions of blame, judgement and criticism.

I listen uncritically to others.

I do not criticize myself.

I taste of many wonderful delights and do not sink into terrible depths.

A Path of Peace with God

I keep myself in a receptive state.

I delight thoroughly in the good things in life.

I am not critical of other people's delight.

I am satisfied by the small, good things in life.

I trust God.

I know my good intentions shine clearly through to people.

I am keeping up this great commitment to myself.

There is no point in holding on to old negative stuff.

I see God's light in the things people say and do.

I am at peace with all others and how they choose to live their life.

I feel deep warmth, peace and contentment in my heart.

I am seeing everything in a truly new light.

I release any prejudice within me and affirm the goodness in all others.

I have no use for complaining about things that cannot be changed.

I bless the experiences of the past and go forth with newer and greater awareness.

Today I become even happier and lighter in my being.

I move through this day in radiant light.

I am staying with good words.

Support. Understanding. Acknowledgment. Praise. Improvement. Appreciation. Encouragement. Growth. Agreement.

I generate life force each morning through spontaneous and loving affirmation.

I move through this day in total peace. I completely accept others. I completely accept myself. I gain strength knowing God is by my side always.

I acknowledge and express fully the tremendous power I have.

I do not force anything. I hold hands with God and let him take me through life.

I maintain this presence with God throughout the day.

Thoughts of God bring me peace and regeneration.

The good intention of others is totally obvious to me.

I illuminate and make clear the great bond of connectedness between others and myself.

I see how others quickly participate with me in the desire to please.

I feel a close connection to the people around me.

I stay focused on the good elements of life.

I do not foster a brooding on the bad.

I emphasize togetherness when there are communal challenges.

This is an adventure into the new and previously unknown.

I am loved and protected by the world around me.

A Path of Peace with God

Bad thought. Bless it. Cast it out. Repeat as needed.

The good in every situation is immediately obvious to me.

I give many smiles of understanding.

I happily show a child-like nature to others.

Great Power.
Great Patience.
Great Love.
Great Understanding.

I am surrounded by great abundance.

Intense love and beauty surround me.

I have no problem with thoughts I earlier perceived as injurious.

I use problem thoughts to feed the fire of faith and love.

I have a clear sense of what is right for me.

The sexuality within me is allowed free expression.

I give true deep thanks for the experiences of today.

I let go and remain fully with others without judgment or criticism.

I am giving thanks where it is due... everywhere.

It took huge power to bring me here.

I see love and God in the mutual concern people show for each other.

I am not hurt by others.

I know that I am deeply loved.

I create happiness and trust right now.

I see the deep vulnerability in myself and others.

I create loving energy to lift others up and keep them up.

I am not afraid to see the true glory of God before me.

I cast out all feelings of envy and jealousy.

The power behind me gives me tremendous confidence.

I let others do what they feel they need to do.

I am surrounded by things that keep lifting my spirit higher and higher.

Elevation, light spirit and elation through: acceptance, understanding, realization, discovery, encouragement.

I am completely open to all the joy in the universe.

I do not resist others.

I feel very confident today.

Today great insight and personal revelation come to me.

I receive quick answers to life's questions.

I keep certain promises to myself.

I let negative thoughts go easily.

Today I am moved further past inner struggle into a state of even greater joy.

This is not a time to be reactive.

I see that this world's struggles bring us closer together.

I have a habit of continually observing that which brings love in.

It is not others' doubt but the care between us that I emphasize.

There are two ways to go in this world – up or down. I choose to go up.

The more I go down the less I go up. Then soon I may not know which way is which.

A laugh is a meeting with our child-like nature.

Thinking responsibly gives inner protection.

I rapidly release difficulty by speaking affirmations in my mind and remembering that God helps manage from behind the scenes.

Darkness is tiny against the backdrop of total love.

The more light and good that I see in my world the greater the support that lifts me.

I recognize and emphasize the light that shines forth in others.

All are peaceful and calm around me.

My trust in You is deeper than it has ever been.

All events occur around me like clockwork.

Here is a way out... no fostering the negative.

It is my own personal responsibility to see and continually recreate the delightful aspects of my life. Here is where there is true freedom with God.

I accept and realize fully the total protection I am given.

Total happiness comes from total self-responsibility... thought responsibility.

I find freedom in a healthy response to negative thought.

There is positivity in God's synchronicity.

I move myself higher by affirming our love ceaselessly.

My life is proceeding exactly as it should.

I have a deep positive sense of things.

I feel totally free to express my creativity.

I am not hurt, resentful or harmed by what others say.

I know that I am doing what is right for me.

I have a strong inner confidence.

I am determined and persistent.

I do not get drawn into challenges created by others.

Today great happiness and miracles happen.

I find great joy in agreement.

I change my thoughts in a positive direction.

I feel light and easy moving through the world.

Each day brings me pleasurable and easy events.

I relax fully in this new awareness.

I feel truly free to be myself.

My dreams help integrate this day and prepare me for tomorrow.

With each affirmation I bring more love into the world.

I quickly let go of any internal blame and criticism.

The experiences of today I find truly enlightening.

Simply petting an animal brings love into them and myself.

Each positive statement is a call for love to come forth into the world.

I skip over words and statements that do not contribute positively.

The love all around me is now burning through loud and clear.

I do not hold myself down focusing on the wrong things.

I say a lot of here-and-now statements and with them bring in a lot of good spirit.

I accept whatever thoughts I think and do not blame myself.

I feel strong and powerful and give of this to others.

I keep myself free and stuck on the positive.

The changes I have gone through have been truly miraculous!

Tremendous thanks and blessings are the order of the day.

I see the ocean of care and affection people give to each other.

I am keeping a place of steady happiness inside.

I bravely accept God's sheer intensity in my life.

I am totally happy and healthy.

I have a secret power... changing my mind.

I feel the grand support of the entire universe.

I see joy and intensity emanating from others.

I positively influence and help encourage others to greater freedom.

It is easier to step out of negativity than to ever go back.

Deeper anxiety is a deeper clinging to inner fear.

I maintain a happy place and am not pulled out of it by others.

I see the vulnerability and desire to improve in us all.

A Path of Peace with God

I bring in lots of love today.

I am happy and at peace with myself.

I am careful to keep positive throughout the day.

I see other's beauty even when they do not see it themselves.

I am totally happy where I am right now.

I see how God works to lift others.

Things are working out just perfectly for me right now.

I see the beauty in each environment I am in.

I delight in and appreciate the creativity of others.

I have a profound and lasting confidence in God's support.

I am surrounded by total love and support.

I support, understand and encourage myself.

I stand strong and centered.

The impersonal aspects of this world have no negative influence over me.

I easily dismiss what I cannot change.

I do my best to respond with my best.

I engage with the positive influences in the universe.

I am charged to the brim with positive energy!

I see what I can truly accomplish in this world and what needs to be done to get there.

It is when I change myself that the world changes around me.

I see beauty bursting out all around me!

There is no point in creating and propagating negativity... mistakenly blocking out the light.

I am focused specifically on what helps.

I see many ways but stick to this healthy way.

I easily see thoughts that have not served me well and release them.

God keeps moving me toward a more profound freedom.

I do not blame myself for the things I could not see before.

I receive lasting protection from thought responsibility and trust in God.

All my needs are met right now.

I have no need to worry about money.

I know that I am protected, supported and provided for.

I see God's light shining brightly in the lives of others.

I have no feelings of remorse or regret about the past.

I value the great joy and friendship I have experienced in my past.

I find the positive response to people and events.

Today I experience brilliant radiance.

I walk hand in hand with God today.

I remind myself of our friendship throughout this day.

God speaks to me often through this beautiful world.

I carry Your spark within myself enthusiastically.

I am very patient in God's peace and presence.

God has been seeding and feeding my consciousness!

I experience great freedom and ease of movement today.

I receive everything as a supportive measure from the universe.

I see clearly the support that man has created for himself.

I release any attachment to old negative ways.

God chimes in at the most key moments to show his support.

The more I resist changing myself the more I will perceive resistance from others.

I let others move at their own pace through life.

I have great strength, insight and determination.

I do not force my beliefs on others.

I am easy and comfortable with great currents of energy within me.

I release any injurious thoughts and keep close the good thoughts.

I feel great comfort keeping God's presence with me throughout this day.

I do not let the past control my present or my future.

I am not drawn into others' anger.

Anger directed outward is a misguided attempt to work on the thoughts and feelings within.

I love myself and everything around me.

I do not harm myself. I do not harm anyone in the world.

Today I actively bring love in at every opportunity I see.

I choose to stay focused on the many positives in the world around me.

I see that God supports me and the beautiful world around me.

Positive spontaneous affirmations roll easily through my mind.

I do not leave my positive path.

I feel happy and free from negative repercussions.

I am energetically lifted higher by the beautiful sounds around me.

I do not lose sight of God's love and beauty.

I am bringing in love and happiness with every chance I get.

I know where I am really meant to be.

I am kicking up the life force all around me.

I acknowledge the total love before me.

The more unhealthy thought is released the more the positive nature of things comes into view.

I am interpreting everything in a positive light.

I see great opportunities to choose happiness all the time.

I experience great love being with God.

I generate positive energy first thing this morning.

Each affirmation I think of is a way to increase love force.

I am meant to be a happy person all the time.

I do not foster negativity toward criminals, lawyers, drugs, politicians or environmental pollution.

There are only two choices: to think or not to think positively.

I am filling up on love today.

I am seeing everything in its positive light to stay in the light.

I see when there is fear in others. I see when there is fear in myself and know how to change my response to it.

I do not blame myself or others for minor, trivial things.

I do not feel anger toward those who feel pushed or hurried.

I feel the deep common bond we all share.

I notice people who feel closed to the light and realize how perplexing the mind can be.

My mind is the magnet that attracts or repels events.

I wave good-bye to cynicism.

Others do not convince me of a gloomy future.

I acknowledge the world has negatives but feel free in all its positives.

I fully acknowledge the beautiful, remarkable people that God has surrounded me with.

There is no need to blame oneself or feel ashamed just because change is needed.

I see great care, love and human assistance around every corner.

In each step I see anew the support of God and the care between people.

I help keep others from bringing themselves down.

Negativity toward myself and others is an indulgence I cannot afford.

I feel a deep sense of personal identity and specialness in each person.

Expressing negativity is a departure from a place of total love.

I am focused on making each action and influence a positive one.

My dreams keep me feeling charged and spirited.

A Path of Peace with God

Self-limits can be placed or erased.

I do not let society and others make me believe it is all a swapping game of a little good for a little bad.

My strength is in how I respond to each event today.

The world reflects back to me what I think and feel.

It is by changing myself that I change how the world looks to me.

I react enthusiastically and with understanding to the events that occur around me today.

God's love is a current that always flows even if my thoughts resist it.

I strip away layers of self-covering and see fully the joyful energy coming through me.

I do not blame myself or society for what I could not see before.

I see the changes I need to make within me crystal clear.

I sense when upwellings of energy rise in myself and others.

I see how God's energy is changed by each person into their own unique feelings and actions.

I know that today I will be provided with just what I need to know.

I feel the energy of the earth and everything around me.

I have great strength to release that which does not deserve to be a part of me.

I am safe and protected in the world.

There is no point in getting angry about the one inner fear. I am powerful enough to change the thoughts that cause the fear.

Blame, judgement and criticism create fear within oneself. That fear can then grow while we do not even know.

I remain in a happy place spotting exactly any behaviors that have been pulling me down.

I feel supported by the world around me.

I skip by the negative and stick with what is positive.

Love moves to the background when blame, judgement and criticism enter the picture.

I care deeply for others.

I see God's great cosmic synchronicity before me all the time.

Changing myself is the best way to change the world.

I have a choice to drop any of the thoughts I am unhappy with.

Everything is going as planned.

I love God.

I am totally comfortable with myself and others.

I am given what truly pleases me.

I am at home in all places.

I receive great help from others.

I know the best actions to take in my life.

I see God in others.

I feel an inner guidance strongly.

I cannot be moved from my place of understanding.

My positive outlook cannot be taken from me.

Each day strengthens me even further in my positive position.

I realize how at home I feel when I feel laughter and love inside me.

I have no doubt of God's support.

I freely release old thought patterns that do not suit me.

My head is a constant stream of affirmations.

I exist to be open and free.

God's kingdom plays beautifully for me today.

God surrounds me with all the glory that he is.

I feel the magnificence in every person I see.

I do not feed the fear in others.

I am proud of what I have accomplished.

The power I have is totally trusting God.

I know what I must do to establish success.

All negative emotions are unique interpretations of the one fear.

Greed, paranoia, hate, desperation, hopelessness, worry, stubbornness, dependency, grudges, rage, pessimism, cynicism and all other negative thoughts and emotions are all branches of the tree of fear.

Positive action toward others helps keep the inner feelings positive.

No element of truth is kept from me.

Time for a personal liberation... the solution: affirmation!

I know the universe reflects back to me my own ability to love myself.

The world is a construction of cooperation and care.

The glorious joy of heaven is distilled in me through music, touch, taste, people, animals, nature, synchronicity.

I receive continual and unending messages from God encouraging me along my path.

I delight in each little message I spot and thank God for the joy there is in our togetherness.

I choose how much love I bring into my life and where I go to get it.

I bring in lots of love at every opportunity I see.

I have a choice to be peaceful, positive and powerful all of the time.

I do not dwell negatively on anybody else, past or present.

I use words that empower people and avoid words that may spread or increase a feeling of fear.

I encourage people to resolve old feelings that are harbored toward others from the past.

I find the positive in each event of today.

I emphasize our thankfulness toward each other and minimize the negative.

I am very worthy of being given great love and reward.

I am happy where I am in God's love.

I know that God intends the best for me.

I do not fuel challenges offered by others.

Outward struggle with others reflects an inner struggle within oneself.

I cast out all feelings of discouragement and know that great things are coming.

I do not interfere with other people's rate of growth.

Seeing aloofness and skepticism in others reminds me of the importance of keeping an open mind.

Fear is a reminder of how important it is to have a strong relationship with God.

I have no fear of rejection from others.

These affirmations are personal truths leading me out of the resistant aspects of my own inner mind.

I must remain free.

I stay focused on more thanks, more hugs and more ways to bring love in.

I am willing to give up my own resistance so that I can become even happier and healthier.

Unpleasant internal mental pictures are visualizations of the one fear.

I feel the joy of laughter and music and know that this is love rising within me.

God has brought me to this place so I can see him more clearly.

Fear, like love, peaks when inner energy levels peak.

A Path of Peace with God

I do not fear the force of love when it rises up within me.

I see how energy is continually delivered by God into each body and the entire universe. This energy is the electricity that keeps the universe turned on.

Inner fear rises in response to the rise of life-sustaining energy provided by God.

Fears pull down the energy that tries to rise freely up through the body.

The more self-change is refused the greater fear becomes and the harder God's force will have to be resisted.

There is only one fear that resists the one inner force of love as it rises up through the body.

Fear is the one feeling of being separated from love.

I know energy is easily stirred up nowadays and when I feel it rise I am not surprised that some fear may come along with it.

Behind the resistance of others is energy seeking to come through.

God is the generator lighting up the universe.

I am surrounded by highly positive people.

I feel deeply loved.

I easily accept all people.

I quickly know when I am feeling the fear in others.

I maintain a high and happy place.

I am patient with myself and the world around me.

A Path of Peace with God

I fill up empty time and space with thoughts of God.

I do not pull myself down by expressing negative comments.

I quickly spot the statements made by others that increase fear. I feel strengthened by my observation and remain unwilling to feed the feeling.

The positive energy within me finds full expression.

There is nothing limiting me now.

The joy of heaven is all around me.

Life energy is fueling my positive outlook.

I am immune to the fear in others.

It is easy for me to adapt to new environments.

I feel happy when I notice people being free around me.

I openly show affection to others.

Generosity is obvious all around me.

Constant affirmation constantly splashes love on the face.

Lots of affirmations produce lots of love.

Lots of thanks and laughter create lots of love.

I see how fear is transmitted like a virus through words and actions.

Degrees of hurt felt inside represent degrees of fear and resistance to inner change.

The more love allowed to pour in, the faster the transformation.

One need:	love
One decision:	change
One negativity:	fear
One solution:	affirmation.

I will not let fear or denial keep me from necessary change.

I am not taking any time off from caring thoughts and actions.

I make a conscious choice to look at my thoughts and actions and keep them in a good place.

I feel liberated avoiding blame toward the impersonal.

The city is a construction of mutual support for each other.

I stand tall and strong when the energy of God comes on.

In energy and light is the truth of resolution.

By positive talk and action I get the most from each experience.

Stopping the blame stops the madness.

God's force seeks to move me past the ways I keep myself down.

Even the slightest thoughts and actions can stir up life force. I do not allow any little fear kicked up along with it to grow.

The one life force moves through me without hindrance, free and clear.

Blame is an indulgence I cannot afford.

I do not fear the happy state I am being moved toward.

I know that this world mirrors my state of happiness and also my resistance to changing myself.

I am not pulled down by the stress in others.

I see how I myself have caused things to happen.

My thoughts leave me feeling happy.

Outward directed anger shows inner pain.

I am totally myself when I am most happy.

Fighting with fear and negativity is a losing battle.

I quickly spot the people who handle fear in a clean and efficient manner.

All negativity is a mask of the one fear.
I have huge power to overcome it!

I do not fear God's tremendous force within me.

I have a pact to not blame myself now and in the future.

Just seeing when fear comes up is a lot of the problem solved.

Two things in this world: good and that which fears to make itself good.

The good force lifts up. Personal fears pull down.

I consciously create happiness in my world.

I instantly know the level of fear around me.

Each day I gain a greater awareness and understanding of myself and the world.

I am not shaken by any level of fear.

I confidently go forth with total trust in God.

A Path of Peace with God

No fear can shake this trust I have in You.

I have no fear of seeing the fear in others.

The beautiful spark of God in all people comes shining through to me.

I see the deep and personal beauty in everyone around me.

I openly thank people for even the small courtesies that are done for me.

I am peaceful and loving with myself.

I love to do what is asked of me and to help others.

I am relaxed and steady in this new way.

One measure of success: inner happiness.

I emphasize the positive aspects of a situation to those around me.

There is inner negativity from blaming society and the endless perpetuation of fear.

Sharing in blame that people have for a person passes fear along.

Fear spreads among society through negative talk and blame toward others.

Seemingly innocent criticisms of society, government, historical events, etc. foster a subtle feeling of victimization and futility deeper down inside oneself.

Fear breeds an inner feeling of powerlessness to change the world.

I feel acknowledged for the work I have done and the work I am now doing.

I have tremendous gratitude toward God.

The penalty of fear can be deep and severe...
this is reason alone not to entertain it.

My way out of fear is turning on the light of inner change and friendship with God.

I accept the speed at which life's events unfold.

I do not feel stranded or isolated in the world.

I accept the past as necessary for my development.

I see the tremendous desire to grow everywhere around me.

I witness humanity's great desire to heal and accept its point of progress now.

Happiness breeds happiness. Fears attract more fears.

I know that within me is great personal truth.

I am resilient and unshaken when others send me their fear.

I feel free to bring in God's light without restriction.

Life force moves through my body like music.

I feel God's life force moving through me and all around me.

I have arrived at a place of peace. I will stay here with God.

I see the sea of support consistently around me showing me the way.

We walk together in peace today.

I do not choose anger. I choose to view the sea of loving support around me and the results of my own decisions.

I eliminate my fear and feel how truly supported I am.

I overcome fear with positivity and gratitude.

As fears were inserted into me I pull them back out.

Staying positive keeps the spirit raised and keeps the good things coming.

When there is life force there is life.

God encourages me toward profound joy.

I am prepared for even more incredible realities.

Resistance to change fosters deeper fear and greater entanglements.

The great ranges of human emotion are truly amazing. I choose to stay with happiness and all its many forms as the consistent basis for myself.

I decide what seeds to plant in the field of my mind.

I feel love rise up with the little things we do for each other.

I do not interfere with others and how they choose to think and feel.

The more God sends energy blasts the less I resist.

I minimize the amount of fear I produce in others.

I see how fear produced in others can grow within them.

I am focused on careful thoughts about a caring world.

I get a lift from the courtesy of others.

A fearful state is not an option for me.

I relax when I feel the rise of God's intense energy.

The joy in others' laughter chimes in me as well.

I am free to fully express my best abilities.

Right now I listen to other peoples' truth.

I am highly sensitive to my mind's changing energy levels.

I know that conscientiousness is called for in every situation I am in.

I let my spirit roam free and bring love and power into my life.

I walk relaxed and comfortable knowing God is all around me.

The wonderful, beautiful spark that You are shines forth in brilliant radiance today.

There is one fear and a million and one disguises.

I take everything in stride today.

I place high value on bringing the spirit up in those around me.

A Path of Peace with God

I do not dance with others when it is the seductive dance of their fear.

I am gentle in the presentation of my ideas.

I listen to others uncritically.

I adapt easily to the desires of others.

I do not blame myself.

I am listened to and respected by others.

I have no need to convince others of my own way.

I rest easy on my own knowing.

I move higher and higher and let my fears drop further and further away.

A Path of Peace with God

I am patient when I see that a person wants to be heard.

I release any blame toward my dad.
I release any blame toward my mom.

I part with people on a happy note.

The joy in others brings me to a whole new level.

I love God. I love the world. I love the people in the world.

Blaming is not an option.

I am staying out of fear. I am staying out of struggle.

I see the underlying desire of others to resolve and amend.

I move through this day in total harmony with my surroundings.

A Path of Peace with God

There is a unique and special beauty in everything I see.

I know what is right for me.

I am strongly connected to the earth.

I know that God loves me.

I see the desire for good health in us all.

I shake hands with God in partnership.

I am patient and understanding of my mom.
I am patient and understanding of my dad.

My entire being is filled with these new affirmations.

I am shown great respect by God.

I do not fear my own strength and the full expression of it.

I feel God's presence with me ceaselessly.

Fear is a weakness I cannot afford to entertain.

I release any stubbornness within me.

I am fluid and offer no resistance to the events occurring around me.

I am patient knowing that events unfold at their proper rate.

I do not doubt God's total support.

I know our friendship is everlasting.

I do not have to look very far to see God's support.

A Path of Peace with God

Continually positive words pull me even closer to the positive inner world I am creating.

I am comfortable feeling God's exciting energy pulsing through me.

I value happiness too much to slip into fear just when something seems not to go right.

I maintain a light and easy atmosphere around me.

My trust in God is built on the strongest foundation.

I trust how God is guiding me and I trust how God is guiding others.

Positive expression toward others keeps me moving toward freedom.

I feel the sweetest sensualities today.

I work in harmony with God.

I gently express my viewpoint.

No more of the trying-to-change-other-people approach.

I go confidently forward knowing God's presence is always with me.

I avoid words that cause people to feel angry at the world.

I am deeply loved and greatly supported by God.

I see and appreciate what God has done for me in my past.

I am aware of God's presence first thing each morning.

I have great faith and trust in God.

I do not direct anger or resentment toward people.

I quickly spot the statements that qualify as pure positivity.

God's energy is a pulse moving through all of creation.

Fear can arise in response to God's powerful energy moving through the body.

I am transported to brilliant inner and outer worlds.

The more I laugh and stay happy the less the world's difficulties influence me.

The design of a butterfly is enough to convince me that the higher joyous places are here on Earth.

I feel God's emanation moving through creation and through my body.

I do not fight against my higher guiding self.

My affirmations lift me up and take me to places where I find even more love.

I realize God's powerful brand of happiness around me and within me.

I am brought the best things in life.

The outer world is a mirror of my inner world.

I do not block the free flow of love through the world.

Fear is one level I restrict my mind's travel to.

It is not being conceited or imposing on others to search for God's presence everywhere.

Nothing upsets the serene patience I get from filling the time with our togetherness.

God communicates with me through the subtle language of my creative mind.

Laugher and love emerge out of empty space itself.

Taste, music, laughter, ecstasy, joyous touch...
God's love bursting forth from the deepest realms within.

Throughout the day I see clearly the particular encounters that really raise energy levels.

I feel satisfied simply being in God's presence.

So many beautiful people and things surround me!

I let God's energy flow easily through me and past me.

God's light is so bright, his energy so strong...
no resisting him in fear.

I feel how God moves through people like the wind moves through the world.

I appreciate the love I receive from You.

I feel rewarded for the hard work I have done.

I feel God's love very close to me.

I am accepted by the people around me.

I do not feel stubborn or pessimistic. The goal is to overcome these feelings.

God is a good friend always right here beside me.

I see people working together to create a better place.

I feel God's magic guiding me through life in a positive direction.

Love is a current we can swim with or against.

Each person accepts information at her or his own rate.

Happiness is as real as fear with a choice in between them.

A Path of Peace with God

I am content with keeping ideas to myself when this is best.

Everything is unfolding at the perfect rate.

It is easy for me to get my needs met.

There is plenty of this world's good to go around.

I am given lots of love and affection.

I am surrounded by order and stability.

I feel blessed having uncovered new knowledge from deep within me.

It is easy to express myself.

I am positive no matter what the opinions of others are.

I bring to me that which makes me happiest.

My base to come back to is positive expression toward others.

I see good intent behind God's messages.

I do not regret any opportunity that I have missed.
What's done is done.

I rise above all divisiveness within me.

I feel supported and cared for by God.

I am blessed with many displays of God's living support and trust.

I am overjoyed with simple pleasures.

For me there is either crossing the bridge with God or staying with fear.

I do not allow myself to pile difficulty on top of difficulty.

The knowledge of how to liberate myself is available to me.

Hate is an impulse I do not give in to.

I know my mother loves me.

My mother will always be there for me.

I have patience and know that I am right where I should be right now.

Blame toward others creates within oneself the feeling of being a victim

I have no use for being angry at the beliefs of others.

I keep God's presence with me always.

God chimes in at the most key moments to show his support.

I release my fear and give in totally to God.

I let the God force rise freely through me.

Each thought has an effect on the world.

Fear, I cast you out. I praise God.

I feel very close to God. I know my needs are important to him.

I trust in the events that are happening around me.

A Path of Peace with God

God is with me every step of the way.

I have maintained the incredible changes within myself!

I feel the joy of companionship in my heart.

I feel deep reward and satisfaction knowing God is there for me always.

I see when a statement comes clearly under the heading of positivity.

I feel loved and warmly accepted by the people around me.

God is very responsive to my needs and wants.

I welcome God into my life as a helpful force.

It is no use continually repeating old complaints.

I am safe, secure and protected.

I see how frequently others reach out to me.

I stay focused on my goals.

I am excited about the power God and I share together.

I feel God's love bursting forth around me in synchronicity.

I patiently repeat affirmations in my mind and know that I am establishing a completely new way forever more.

Affirmations bring positivity up around me making it hard for fear to penetrate.

I release all limits on the amount of love I can bring in.

It is good thoughts that bring the real rewards.

A Path of Peace with God

I take charge of my life by taking charge of my thoughts.

I move quickly out of environments I know are not right for me.

I stay unattached to the results of my work.

I am gentle and caring with others.

I feel acknowledged, honored and rewarded.

I appreciate the support I am given in life right now.

I feel strong knowing God is at my side always.

I feel at peace with God.

I know that God is there every instant and up ahead around every corner.

A Path of Peace with God

Feelings we feel about others remain within ourselves.

Pulling out of difficulty with others is pulling out of difficulty with oneself.

I adapt through cooperation... with God, with others and with myself.

It is wonderful to start anew and let the past go completely.

I let people move out of my life if necessary. I know I am supported.

A little bit of fear signals not to go into big fear.

I am very aware of God's presence around me.

I cannot lose the power I have been given.

I maintain and continue this joyful state of mind.

I easily suspend my own opinions.

The life I have created is just right for me.

I harbor no self-criticism when I make a mistake.

I am patiently writing my way into freedom.

No entering into the next level of fear.

When the energy steps up I do not step my fear up along with it.

God is reasonable in what he asks of me.

God's creativity speaks to me through my mind and the world outside me.

I choose thoughts that allow love to enter.

The work I have done has made big changes.

I share with God the joy I feel.

I feel happy and successful.

I feel free of fear. I feel free of inner negativity.

I move away from negativity easily.

We work as a team.

I move easily into an awareness of God.

I am surrounded by waterfalls that keep carrying my fears far away.

Negative thought is the wrapping on fear.

No blame, no judgment, no criticism. We can move past it.

I bring relief into my life.

I am happy to have God with me every step of the way.

I value the experiences I have had in the past.

I stay happy and committed to God.

I keep focused on the togetherness we share.

Even the slightest synchronicities bring me to an awareness of God.

I cannot help seeing God behind everything.

I stay loving and generous with others and myself.

God is creatively showing that he supports me.

God is behind the empty space and everything that fills it.

God is working behind the scenes sending love at certain times and helping to guide me in certain directions.

I have the knowledge to really move myself forward now.

I sit confidently with this new knowledge I have learned.

A Path of Peace with God

The little events going on around me are little hints of what is going on within me.

I realize that I make the decisions in my life.

I feel a close kinship with God.

Affirmations help bring fear out to be dissipated.

I have God to help guide me through the important decisions.

God brings meaning to even the little events in my life.

Blame is self-disempowerment.

I take full responsibility for the direction my life takes.

I accept God's unending presence in my life.

I see the vulnerability in others and stand clear of impulsiveness.

It is great laughing fear away just when it starts to show up.

God is a quiet participant that I make important in my life.

I will keep moving past my boundaries and moving past any fear that arises within my mind.

I reflect support and stability back to others.

I take full responsibility for how I respond to life.

Thanking is therapeutic.

I am willing to let God help me past fear.

I feel God with me every step of the way.

A Path of Peace with God

Everything affirms something.

God has brought me to a good place.

Positive statements carry love with them and negative statements carry fear.

I see the care behind the concern.

I move higher and higher and let my fears drop further and further away.

I am not afraid of the strength that affirmations generate.

I feel no need to react to the fear in others.

God is a force I keep coming back to.

God openly shows himself to me.

Life is an affirmation of mine that has become a reality.

I see signatures of God all around me.

I have learned a secret... not complaining.

Part of me sees my limit and is helping me past it.

How I treat myself is a priority to God.

I have moved past the times in my life when I did not see a choice.

I can create my own survival or allow my own demise.

God is a patient whisper of reassurance.

I have gained a great inner strength that cannot be taken from me.

A Path of Peace with God

These positive feelings cannot be kept down anymore.

There is a strong inner power within me.

I am creating a sense of fairness in my world.

The strides we have made together are incredible!

God values my partnership with him.

My greatest accomplishment is peace with God and myself.

Life mirrors the portrait we paint of ourselves.

I see the big changes I have made and know that results will come.

There is a presence behind all expression.

I trust God with each moment.

I am stuck on the thoughts I have found that have saved me.

I feel confident knowing the world can be influenced through thought.

I can choose to trust the Spirit with each moment or follow the many ups and downs that fear has to offer.

God knows the good things I need and want and is helping to take me there.

I openly show my appreciation to others.

I repeat a single affirmation for days or much longer to bring the strength I need to myself.

I keep returning to a place of understanding with God.

The letter "T" is for Trust.

Justified or not, blame isn't healthy.

I graciously accept where I am right now.

The external world is a part of me.

Patient trust rather than impulsive fear.

I trust myself to have a steady, calm response to fear if it rises within me.

Thank You for the strength that saves me.

Blame is not worth the price.

I gain the courage to keep affirming who I am and what I dream for.

I value this friendship with You.

I have found an easy solution with God.

Instead of counting up all the bad I keep trusting in the good.

Love is the huge standard we are held to.

A place of non-anger toward others is the best place for me.

I am being conditioned to sustain greater love.

I feel rewarded, satisfied and acknowledged.

Constructive change without fear.

Other people's anger does not need to be my anger.

A Path of Peace with God

I keep causing my good thoughts to come up.

I acknowledge the good work God's invisible force keeps doing for me.

I have the advantage of seeing and accepting God's presence in my life.

The mind's attractive force is as real as any magnet.

There is no use getting upset over the opinion of another.

God is a good force to me. God is a supportive force to me. God is a protective force to me. God is a loving force to me.

God's support is getting through to me.

I trust myself not to stay in fear long.

To get where I want to be I need to be patient now.

Thoughts are very sensitive instruments.

God is taking me to his higher, lighter state of mind.

I resolve to trust in God rather than running with fear and what it can do.

The beautiful things outside represent the beautiful thoughts inside.

Social action without fear and anger.

Anger gets misdirected so it is better avoided.

God is a single flutist playing from behind the backdrop of all people and things.

I feel the presence of love moving the world around me.

Thoughts and actions carry either love or fear behind them.

I keep a commitment with God. I keep a good space with God.

Love is the high standard and fear is the breakaway point.

Fear likes to be overdramatic and anger premature.

Giving in to fear is like leaving one's feelings to the whims of a child.

Some thoughts should never be let go of.

My big advantage is trusting God.

Fear is a reality that keeps dreams from reality.

I feel God's influence strongly in my life but know that I am the one who directs it.

I trust my mind and my ability to balance my strengthening with some tranquility.

I stay close to the light to get past fear.

There is only one decision: to go with or against love's current.

I let go of any fear and create a space so love can come in.

Nobody else can create self-change.

Through forgiveness and gratitude I free myself of the past.

There is nobody to blame for where my own fear has taken me.

I trust and appreciate God.

It is resolution and reassurance that I will keep coming back to.

God is present and helping.

I walk in peace and partnership with God today.

I have to just relax and move with time.

I am grounded and centered within my body.

I feel sexually fulfilled and satisfied.

I know God is happy with me.

I still need to support myself even when the outer world does not reflect this.

I have the strength it takes to not collaborate with fear.

Name-calling won't work.

I move through this day in a loving place with God.

I am playful and easy with God and others.

I have to find my own truth.

I leave old lessons behind and find a new way.

My jaw is relaxed, my hands are relaxed and my mind is open.

The body knows when fear has entered.

It is not knowing who to criticize… it is not criticizing at all.

I value the communication I have with God.

I am anchored in my body. I am rooted to the earth.

Words are suggestions that the mind sees and feels. Harsh words cause the mind to sample harsh feelings.

I stay positive with God. I stay positive with others.

I am pleasantly supported in life.

I gracefully accept the good things coming to me.

I let go of challenge I perceive from others and embrace new resolve.

Unending affirmation is one answer to the keys that time keeps to itself for now.

I win when upset is reduced.

I will keep finding my own knowledge and establishing a healthy way for myself.

Today I am relaxed, I am peaceful and I am strong.

I have my own strength and power now.

God's invisibility brings out my own strength and answers.

Affirmations saturate every cell of my body.

Each word or gesture of anger avoided is a point earned.

I am strongest when I am in a calm place.

Now is the time to be strong.

The power is there; I just have to learn how to harness it.

I let love flow easily up and through me.

I find signs of God's support all around me today.

The more I move forward the more boldly God's presence shows itself to me.

It is a time of forgiveness now.

The pattern is there; I have only to let the seed unfold.

I trust God.

I choreograph good thoughts and repeat them ad infinitum.

I carefully place thoughts today.

I depend on God. I rely on God.

Affirmations help keep the doors from closing on the positive energy moving through me.

I come to conclusions that are worth being attached to.

Calmness strengthens my truth.

God freely offers his love to me.

I let go of stubbornness. I let go of sarcasm.

It is time to relax and go more easily now.

I am walking an easy path with God.

God is a source of resolution in my life.

Affirmation repetition is an exercise in strength, mind control and free will.

I am grateful to God.

I trust God to help build me to sustain his energy.

It is not a time to get too upset when I meet up with the results of a decision I have made.

I am not surprised when I see the positive results that come from trusting God.

I superimpose good thoughts.

I am proud of the sure way I have found with God.

It is not insensitive to stay strong and unaffected in fearful times.

I rest knowing trust brings an underlying order.

I have moved into a happy, joyous space with God.

I am strong and happy in a spirited place with God.

I am the one that lives with the feelings I direct toward others.

Good-bye old friend. Your beautiful spirit will always be with me.

I walk a steady, knowing path with God today.

I keep a proud, positive place with God.

God is a strong force. God is on my side.

Change or fear: the choice is mine.

I am in a trusting place with God.
I am in a hopeful place with God.

I see miracles today.

I have achieved victory.

I am tenacious and resilient.

I am well provided for.

I am free to express, free to create and free to reveal.

I move with the position that orchestrates.

I feel acknowledged by God.

I feel recognized, supported and well compensated.

Now is a time to be tolerant and diplomatic.

I have found a peaceful place of no blame.

I keep a proud trust with God.

I move with God's design.

I stay hopeful and light-spirited with God.

I have reached a calm place of knowing.

I am free to live life as I choose.

I keep a calm, empowered state.

I am free, I am independent and self-sufficient.

God wants me to have the tools that change the mind, that bring his wealth.

I have an agreement with God.

Now is not a time to let fear have its way with me.

Affirmations bring strength to good intentions.

I give thanks to God.

I am very thankful and appreciative.

A smile on the face seals the affirmation even more strongly.

Thank You for Your guidance.

To sustain great love requires overcoming great fear.

Affirmations help take fear away and let God's energy blast through.

God has been a good friend to me.

Affirmations send a vibration that moves throughout the mind and body.

Affirmations keep me grounded as God's energy pulses through.

Now is a time of great peace and abundance. I am giving many thanks.

Affirmations seed the subconscious mind and then grow back to the surface.

I have found a way to sustain strength.

I end this day with many thanks to God.

I instantly recognize God all around me.

A Path of Peace with God

God's wish is that I benefit from his higher knowledge.

God is making himself known to me.

Fear... the cost of independence? It shows the mind where not to go.

I feel safe with God at my side.

God's strength and knowledge are available to me.

God is grateful. God is appreciative.

God's guidance gets easily through to me.

God appreciates and values my friendship with him.

God is kind and reasonable in his expectations of me.

Hate is not a good place for me. I see my choices clearly.

Now is not a time to dance with fear.

There is no need to be angry or upset now.

I am set up for success.

I choose to be positive and uplifted today.

I am consciously creating my own reality.

I joyfully express love and gratitude to others.

I go quickly with others when their suggestion is to move out of fear.

I feel privileged to have this intimacy with You.

A Path of Peace with God

It is time to give up the resistance.

God is there in the tough times.

God freely offers his love, strength and knowledge to me.

In these tests of my strength I stand tall.

God is good. God is strong. God is kind.

These affirmations are keys I cannot lose.

I keep to a place of joy and understanding with God.

There is no use blaming others when the results of my own
decisions arrive.

Thank you for Your assistance.

I win when I keep my strength.

I rejoice in the free expression of others.

It is better not to let fear get carried away with me.

I let others be the way they choose to be.

Now is not a time to bring myself down because of other people's choices.

I am cruising in accordance with the cosmos.

It is better to keep a calm trust right now.

I feel the sweetest sensualities today.

It would be a shame if I were to bring myself down from my own good place because of somebody else's truth.

A Path of Peace with God

155

I choose not to give my power and happiness away if I see old patterns arise.

God is a good friend of mine.

I trust God to come through for me.

Now is not a time to put up a resistance to God's energy moving through me.

I freely express myself to God.

I like to color my mind with affirmations.

God's energy current flows easily through me unrestricted.

God takes good care of me.

I wish well upon all others in the world.

God is honorable. God is kind. I thank God.

I feel safe with God.

God accepts me unconditionally.
God loves me unconditionally.

I accept God unconditionally.
I love God unconditionally.

I move into a space of knowing and right guidance.

Index

beliefs, 57, 64, 113

betrayed, 2

biochemistry, xxix

blame, 1-4, 8, 14, 19, 20, 22, 24, 25, 27, 29, 32, 33, 49, 50, 55, 61, 62, 65, 66, 82, 83, 85, 89, 96, 97, 122, 130, 135, 149

blessings, 22, 25, 27, 35, 50, 110, 111

boundaries, 125

brood, 37

C

calm, 46, 130, 143, 149, 155

care, 1, 9, 14, 20, 33, 44, 50, 63, 66, 74, 82, 94, 111, 116, 126, 156

careful, 1, 9, 14, 52, 94, 144

centered, 53, 136

challenge, 1, 37, 48, 76, 138

change, 7, 26, 27, 30, 35, 48, 50, 53, 54, 61, 62, 64-67, 78, 81-83, 90, 92, 93, 101, 114, 121, 128, 131, 135, 147, 149

charged, 53, 63, 116

child-like, 38, 45, 134

choice, 2, 61, 67, 75, 82, 109, 127, 147, 153, 155

choose, 2, 9, 33, 35, 45, 59, 60, 74, 92, 93, 121, 129, 149, 153, 155, 156

clear, 10, 17, 23, 26, 30, 34, 37, 41, 49, 56, 64, 77, 83, 108, 114, 125, 153

comfortable, 57, 58, 67, 95, 100

commitment, 34, 134

communication, 107, 137

community, 22

companionship, 114

compensated, 148

complain, 35, 114, 127

compliment, 8, 23

concern, 20, 42, 126

confidence, 11, 13, 21, 29, 43, 47, 53, 85, 101, 123, 129

connectedness, 10, 37, 98

hands, 36, 56, 98, 137
happiness, 6, 14, 18, 25, 26, 28, 29, 31, 35, 38, 42, 46, 48, 50, 51, 52, 59, 60, 61, 67, 75, 77, 79, 81, 83-85, 89, 91, 93, 97, 100, 106, 109, 111, 121, 122, 136, 147, 156
harm, 47, 58
harmony, 97, 101
hate, 32, 73, 112, 153
health, 30, 31, 46, 51, 54, 60, 77, 98, 130, 139
heart, 5, 35, 114
heaven, 13, 74, 80
hostility, 10, 26

I

ideas, 31, 96, 110
immune, 80
impatience, 7
impersonal, 53, 82
independent, 149
indulgence, 63, 83
insight, 24, 29, 43, 57
intention, 34, 37, 150, 152
intimacy, 153
isolated, 90

J

jaw, 4, 137
jealousy, 42
joy, 4, 8, 11, 12, 18, 24, 28, 29, 31, 43, 44, 48, 51, 55, 64, 74, 77, 80, 92, 94, 97, 106, 107, 111, 114, 118, 121, 147, 153, 154
judgement, 24, 29, 33, 41, 66, 122

K

kind, 152, 154, 157
knowing, 14, 21, 36, 60, 95, 96, 99, 101, 114, 116, 129, 137, 146, 147, 149, 157

O

opinion, 110, 118, 132
opportunity, 5, 58, 60, 74, 111

P

partnership, 7, 98, 128, 136
past, 1, 2, 9, 11, 17, 25, 35, 55, 58, 75, 83, 91, 105, 117, 122, 135
path, 2, 3, 18, 33, 59, 74, 145, 147
patience, 7, 38, 107, 112
patterns, 1, 2, 12, 72, 144, 156
peace, 2, 4, 9, 10, 13, 24, 25, 29, 35, 36, 46, 52, 56, 75, 86, 92, 116,
    128, 136, 139, 149, 151
perfect, 4, 32, 52, 110
persistence, 47
pessimism, 73, 109
playful, 137
pleasure, 28, 111
politics, 60
positive, 18, 33, 46, 48-53, 55, 59-63, 66, 71-73, 75, 79, 80, 83, 89,
    92, 100, 105, 109-111, 114, 115, 126, 128, 138, 145, 146, 147,
    153
power, 10, 12, 22, 25, 27, 32, 33, 36, 38, 42, 43, 50, 51, 66, 73, 75,
    84, 90, 95, 105, 106, 115, 117, 124, 128, 143, 149, 156
praise, 3, 14, 17, 36, 113
prejudice, 35
presence, 36, 56, 58, 99, 101, 105, 107, 108, 113, 117, 124, 128,
    132, 134, 144
present, 58, 75, 136
promise, 44
protection, 1, 3, 9, 11, 24, 37, 45, 46, 55, 65, 115, 132
proud, 73, 146, 147, 149

Q

R

radiance, 7, 35, 56, 95
rage, 2, 73
reality, 127, 134, 153
reassurance, 127, 136
receptive, 34
regeneration, 36
regret, 55, 111
rejoice, 155
relax, 48, 89, 94, 95, 136, 137, 139, 145
release, 1, 2, 9, 11, 17, 19, 26-28, 35, 45, 54, 58, 60, 65, 72, 97, 99,
    113, 115
remorse, 55
resentment, 23, 30, 31, 47, 105
resilient, 91, 148
resistance, 9, 43, 57, 64, 77-79, 81, 83, 93, 94, 99, 105, 108, 154,
    156
resolution, 32, 82, 136, 145
resolve, 9, 10, 75, 97, 133, 138
respect, 96, 98
responsibility, 2, 14, 45, 46, 55, 124, 125
restriction, 28, 91, 107, 156
revelation, 43
reward, 26, 75, 108, 114-116, 131
rooted, 138

S

safe, 9, 65, 115, 152, 157
sarcasm, 145
satisfied, 7, 28, 34, 108, 114, 131, 136
secure, 115
seed, 56, 93, 144, 151
sensualities, 100, 155
separation, 78
sexuality, 41, 136

shame, 27, 62, 155
sincerity, 8
smile, 5, 14, 38, 150
space, 11, 21, 29, 80, 107, 123, 134, 135, 147, 157
spirit, 5, 11, 17, 24, 43, 50, 63, 92, 95, 129, 147, 149
stability, 110, 125
stranded, 90
strength, 6, 10, 21, 22, 29, 36, 57, 64, 65, 72, 80, 99, 126, 127, 129, 130, 135, 136, 143, 145, 150-152, 154, 155
stress, 84
strong, 47, 50, 53, 71, 76, 82, 98, 100, 108, 116, 135, 139, 143, 146, 147, 150, 154
struggle, 44, 76, 97
stubborn, 73, 99, 109, 145
subconscious, 151
success, 2, 73, 89, 121, 153
support, 3, 4, 20, 23, 36, 45, 51, 53, 55-57, 59, 63, 66, 72, 82, 92, 99, 101, 111, 113, 116, 117, 123, 125, 132, 136, 138, 144, 148
synchronicity, 8, 21, 47, 66, 74, 115, 123

T
taste, 33, 74, 107
team, 122
tenacious, 148
thankfulness, 1, 2, 4, 5, 8, 11, 12, 14, 19, 25, 41, 50, 74, 75, 77, 81, 86, 125, 130, 150, 151, 154, 157
thoughtfulness, 6, 22
thought, 2, 6, 9, 12, 14, 18, 22, 25, 30, 31, 36, 38, 41, 44-46, 48, 50, 54, 55, 58, 60, 64, 66, 67, 72, 80, 82-84, 94, 113, 115, 116, 121, 122, 129, 132-134, 144, 146
today, 23, 24, 28-30, 32, 35, 41, 43, 44, 48, 49, 52, 56, 58, 61, 64, 65, 72, 75, 92, 95, 100, 136, 139, 144, 147, 148, 153, 155
togetherness, 18, 20, 24, 37, 44, 74, 92, 107, 109, 115, 123, 128
tolerant, 148
tranquility, 4, 135

Personal Notes